Tenor
Volume 2

THE
SINGERS
MUSICAL THEATRE
ANTHOLOGY

A collection of songs from the musical stage, categorized by voice type. The selections are presented in their authentic settings, excerpted from the original vocal scores.

Compiled and Edited by Richard Walters

HAL•LEONARD™
CORPORATION
7777 W. BLUEMOUND RD. P.O. BOX 13819 MILWAUKEE, WI 53213

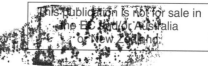

This publication is not for sale in the EC and/or Australia or New Zealand.

ISBN 978-0-7935-2331-3

FOREWORD

As the century nears its end, it is apparent to me that the most important and lasting body of performable American music for singers has come from the musical theatre and musical film. The classical tradition as it has been continued in the United States in this century has produced few major composers who have written extensively for the voice, producing a relatively small body of sometimes profound and beautiful literature, but often relevant only to specialized audiences. In pre-rock era popular traditions, the songs that were not written for the stage or film are largely inferior in quality to those written for Broadway and Hollywood (although there are plenty of exceptions to this general rule). Perhaps the reason is simply that the top talent was attracted to and nurtured by those two venues, and inspired by the best performers. But it's also possible that writing for a character playing some sort of scene, no matter how thin the dramatic context (sometimes undetectable), has inherently produced better songs. Compare a Rodgers and Hart ballad from the 1930s (which are all from musicals) to just an average pop ballad from that time not from the stage or screen, if you can dig one up, and you might see what I mean. Popular music of the rock era, primarily performers writing dance music for themselves to record, is almost a completely different aesthetic, and is most often ungratifying for the average singer to present in a typical performance with piano accompaniment.

The five volumes that comprise the original edition of *The Singer's Musical Theatre Anthology,* released in 1987, contain many of the most famous songs for a voice type, as well as being peppered with some more unusual choices. Volume two of the series allows a deeper investigation into the available literature. I have attempted to include a wide range of music, appealing to many different tastes and musical and vocal needs. As in the first volumes, whenever possible the songs are presented in what is their most authentic setting, excerpted from the vocal score or piano/rehearsal score, in the key originally performed and with the original piano accompaniment arrangement (which is really a representation of the orchestra, of course, although Kurt Weill was practically the only Broadway composer to orchestrate his own shows). A student of this subject will notice that these accompaniments are quite a bit different from the standard sheet music arrangements that were published of many of these songs, where the melody is put into a simplified piano part and moved into a convenient and easy piano key, without much regard to vocal range.

In the first volume of the series, I tried to walk a fine line in the mezzo-soprano choices, attempting to accomodate a mix of how theatre people define that voice type —almost exclusively meaning belting — and how classical tradition defines mezzo-soprano. In volume two I have restricted the choices to songs for a belting range, although they don't necessarily need to be belted, and put any songs sung in what theatre people call "head voice" or "soprano voice" in the soprano volume. As was true in the first volume, classically trained mezzo-sopranos will be comfortable with many of the songs in the soprano book.

The "original" keys are presented here, although that often means only the most comfortable key for the original performer. Transpositions of this music are perfectly acceptable. Some songs in these volumes might be successfully sung by any voice type. Classical singers and teachers using these books should remember that the soprano tessitura of this style of material, which often seems very low, was a deliberate aesthetic choice, aimed at clarity of diction, often done to avoid a cultured sound in a singing voice inappropriate to the desired character of the song and role, keeping what I term a Broadway ingenue range. Barbara Cook and Julie Andrews are famous examples of this kind of soprano, with singing concentrated in an expressive and strong middle voice. Also regarding tessituras, some men may find comfortable songs in both the tenor and baritone volumes, in a "baritenor" range, typically with a top note of G.

It's exciting to present songs in this new edition that have never before appeared in print. Many great songs still hold the stage, even if many of the shows don't. The nine volumes of the series present 358 songs from 117 musicals, dating from 1905 to 1991. It's a small percentage of our theatre heritage, but is still a comprehensive and relatively representative sampling of the stage music of New York, and to a much lesser degree London, in the twentieth century.

Many people have been kind and helpful to me in my research and preparation of this edition. They will forgive me if I only mention my debt of gratitude to the late musical theatre historian Stanley Green. I was fortunate enough to work with him as his editor on his last two books. Stanley's grasp of the subject, his compelling prose, and his high standards of research continue to inspire me.

Richard Walters, editor
May, 1993

THE
SINGER'S MUSICAL THEATRE
ANTHOLOGY
Tenor
Volume 2

Contents

ABOUT THE SHOWS

THE APPLE TREE

Music: Jerry Bock
Lyrics: Sheldon Harnick
Book: Sheldon Harnick, Jerry Bock, Jerome Coopersmith
Director: Mike Nichols
Choreographer: Lee Theodore and Herbert Ross
Opened: 10/18/66, New York; a run of 463 performances

Here was a new concept for Broadway—one musical containing three separate one-act musicals, like Puccini's *Il Trittico* or Offenbach's *Tales of Hoffmann*. Though the stories in *The Apple Tree* have nothing in common and, in fact, could be played separately, they are tied together by interrelated musical themes and by the whimsical reference to the color brown. The first act is based on Mark Twain's *The Diary of Adam and Eve*, and dealt with the dawn of humanity and innocence. The second act is based on Frank R. Stockton's celebrated *The Lady or the Tiger?* in which a warrior's fate, unresolved in the story, was determined by the choice of door he enters. The third act is based on Jules Feiffer's *Passionella*, a fantasy about a poor chimney sweep who became a movie star. "Forbidden Fruit" is sung by the Snake in Act I to tempt the fledgling humans.

BEGGAR'S HOLIDAY

Music: (Edward) Duke Ellington
Lyrics and Book: John Latouche
Director: Nicholas Ray
Choreographer: Valerie Betts
Opened: 12/26/46, New York; a run of 111 performances

At a time when the Brecht-Weill *The Threepenny Opera* was virtually unknown in the U.S. (its fame would await the 1954 production), another musical based on the 1728 play *The Beggar's Opera* played in New York. Updated to present day New York, *Beggar's Holiday* was experimental, unique, and non-formulamatic, and was highly regarded by some critics, but never caught on with the theatre-goers. If it had been a hit, Ellington might have found a comfortable home on Broadway, writing his sophisticated and rich music for the theatre rather than for the concert hall and recordings.

BELLS ARE RINGING

Music: Jule Styne
Book and Lyrics: Betty Comden and Adolph Green
Director: Jerome Robbins
Choreographers: Jerome Robbins and Bob Fosse
Opened: 11/29/56, New York; a run of 924 performances

This musical, written for the star Judy Holliday, is about a meddlesome operator at a telephone answering service, a type of business that existed before voice mail, who gets involved with her clients' lives. She is in fact so helpful to one, a playwright in need of inspiration, that they meet and fall in love. In "I Met a Girl," Jeff tries, unsuccessfully, to contain his feelings of excitement at meeting Ella, whom he doesn't realize is his telephone answering service operator..

The material in this section is by Stanley Green and Richard Walters, some of which was previously published elsewhere.

CABARET

Music: John Kander
Lyrics: Fred Ebb
Book: Joe Masteroff
Director: Harold Prince
Choreographer: Ron Field
Opened: 11/20/66, New York; a run of 1,165 performances

Adapted from Christopher Isherwood's *Berlin Stories* and John van Druten's dramatizaion, *I Am a Camera, Cabaret* used a sleazy Berlin night club as a metaphor for the decadent world of pre-Hitler Germany of the 1930s. Though the story focusses on Sally Bowles, a British expatriate, and her ill-fated affair with Clifford Bradshaw, an American writer, the symbolism of the show is conveyed through an epicene Master of Ceremonies who recreates the tawdry atmosphere of the period through a series of musical numbers at the Kit Kat Club. The score is purposely reminiscent of Weill and Brecht, and starred Weill's widow, Lotte Lenya, in an important role. "Wilkommen" opens the entire show. In 1972 Bob Fosse directed a movie version, which reversed the nationalities of the principals, and used a different storyline.

CALL ME MADAM

Music and Lyrics: Irving Berlin
Book: Howard Lindsay and Russel Crouse
Director: George Abbott
Choreographer: Jerome Robbins
Opened: 10/12/50, New York; a run of 644 performances

President Truman appointed Washington party-giver Perle Mesta to be Ambassador to Luxembourg, and the situation was ripe for being satirized, along with commentary along the way about politics and foreign affairs, and the brash American abroad. Set in the tiny fictional country of Lichtenburg, Sally's unconventional, undiplomatic manner charms them all. This show was written as a star vehicle for Ethel Merman, and was Berlin's longest Broadway run, except for his *Annie Get Your Gun.* Kenneth Gibson is Sally's young aide, in love with the Princess Marie.

CAROUSEL

Music: Richard Rodgers
Lyrics and Book: Oscar Hammerstein II
Director: Rouben Mamoulian
Choreographer: Agnes de Mille
Opened: 4/19/45, New York; a run of 890 performances

The collaborators of *Oklahoma!* chose Ferenc Molnar's Liliom as the basis for their second show and their best score Oscar Hammerstein shifted Molnar's Budapest locale to a late 19th century fishing village in New England. The two principal roles are Billy Bigelow, a carnival barker, and Julie Jordan, an ordinary factory worker. Julie's best friend, Carrie, becomes engaged to Mr. Enoch Snow, and things go temporarily sour in their relationship when Snow believes Carrie to be a trollop— "Geraniums in the Window." They patch things up later.

CHESS

Music: Benny Andersson and Bjorn Ulvaeus
Lyrics: Tim Rice
Book: Richard Nelson, based on an idea by Tim Rice
Director: Trevor Nunn
Choreographer: Lynne Taylor-Corbett
Opened: 4/28/88, New York; a run of 68 performances

There have been musicals about the cold war (*Leave it to Me!, Silk Stockings*), but *Chess* was the first to treat the conflict seriously, using an international chess match as a metaphor. Like *Jesus Christ Superstar* and *Evita, Chess* originated as a successful record album before it became a stage production. The London production was a high tech spectacle, rock opera type presentation. The libretto was revised for New York, and a different production approach was tried. "Someone Else's Story" was added for the Broadway run. The story is a romantic triangle with a Bobby Fischer type American chess champion, a Russian opponent who defects to the West, and the Hungarian born American woman who transfers her affections from the American to the Russian without bringing happiness to anyone. Though the show ran three years in London, it never made back its initial investment there. It lost $6,000,000 in New York.

THE DESERT SONG

Music: Sigmund Romberg
Lyrics: Otto Harbach and Oscar Hammerstein II
Book: Otto Harbach, Oscar Hammerstein II and Frank Mandel
Director: Arthur Hurley
Choreographer: Bobby Connolly
Opened: 11/30/26, New York; a run of 471 performances

One of the best known operettas of the 1920s, *The Desert Song* was the first collaboration between Romberg, Harbach and Hammerstein. Though a swashbuckling romance following conventional lines of the day, the work also contained references to current political events, as well as the hot and popular films of Rudolph Valentino. In the plot, a French woman is abducted into the Sahara by the mysterious Red Shadow, leader of the rebels, but he turns out to really be the son of the Governor of Morocco. The musical was unsuccessfully revived in New York in 1973. Movie versions were released in 1929, 1943, and 1953.

DO RE MI

Music: Jule Styne
Lyrics: Betty Comden and Adolph Green
Book and Direction: Garson Kanin
Choreographers: Marc Breaux and Deedee Wood
Opened: 12/26/60, New York; a run of 400 performances

A wild satire on the ways in which the underworld muscled in on the jukebox business, *Do Re Mi* was adapted by Kanin from his own novel. With characters reminiscent of the raffish denizens of *Guys and Dolls,* the show offered two of Broadway's top clowns of the era: Phil Silvers as a fast-talking, would-be bigshot, and Nancy Walker as his long suffering spouse.

EVITA

Music: Andrew Lloyd Webber
Lyrics: Tim Rice
Director: Harold Prince
Choreographer: Larry Fuller
Opened: 6/23/78, London; a run of 2,900 performances.
    9/25/79, New York; a run of 1,567 performances

Because of its great success in London, *Evita* was practically a pre-sold hit when it began its run on Broadway. Based on the events in the life of Argentina's strong-willed leader, Eva Peron, the musical—with Patti LuPone in the title role in New York—traced her rise from struggling actress to wife of dictator Juan Peron (Bob Gunton), and virtual co-ruler of the country. Part of the concept of the show is to have a slightly misplaced Che Guevera (played by Mandy Patinkin) as a narrator and conscience to the story of Eva's quick, greedy rise to power and her early death from cancer. "On This Night of a Thousand Stars" is the song of a swarmy nightclub singer who is Eva's first conquest. "High Flying, Adored" is sung by Che about Eva after Peron is made president of Argentina.

FANNY

Music and Lyrics: Harold Rome
Book: S. N. Berman and Joshua Logan
Director: Joshua Logan
Choreographer: Helen Tamiris
Opened: 11/4/54, New York; a run of 888 performances

Fanny takes us to the colorful, bustling port of Marseilles "not so long ago" for a musical version of Marcel Pagnol's French film trilogy, Marius, Fanny and César (originally played by Ezio Pinza). Compressed into an evening's entertainment, the action-packed story concerns Marius, who yearns to go to sea; his father, César, the local café owner; Panisse, a prosperous middle-aged sail maker; and Fanny, the girl beloved by both Marius and Panisse. Though Fanny has a child with Marius just before he ships off, Panisse marries her and brings up the boy as his own. When Marius returns demanding both Fanny and his song, César convinces him that Panisse has the more rightful claim. Years later, however, the dying Panisse dictates a letter to Marius offering him Fanny's hand in marriage. All of the songs were eliminated for the 1960 screen version.

FIDDLER ON THE ROOF

Music: Jerry Bock
Lyrics: Sheldon Harnick
Book: Joseph Stein
Director and Choreographer: Jerome Robbins
Opened: 9/22/64, New York; a run of 3,242 performances

An undeniable classic of the Broadway theatre, *Fiddler on the Roof* took a compassionate view of a Jewish community in Czarist Russia, where the people struggled to maintain their traditions and identity in the face of persecution. Despite a story that some thought had limited appeal (it was based on tales by Sholom Aleichem, including "Tevye's Daughters."), the theme struck such a universal response that the Fiddler was perched precariously on his roof for a record of over seven years, nine months. The plot is set in the village of Anatevka in 1905, and tells of the efforts of Tevye, his wife Golde, and their five daughters, to cope with their harsh existence. At the play's end, when a Cossack program has forced everyone out of the village, Tevye and what is left of his family look forward to a new life in America. "Miracle of Miracles" is sung by Motel the tailor, who is Tzeitel's beloved. Tzeitel rebels against the arranged marriage plans for her, and instead Motel tells Tevye that he and Tzeitel are in love and wish to be married. Tevye reluctantly agrees.

FINIAN'S RAINBOW

Music: Burton Lane
Lyrics: E. Y. Harburg
Book: E. Y. Harburg and Fred Saidy
Director: Bretaigne Windust
Choreographer: Michael Kidd
Opened: 1/10/47, New York; a run of 725 performances

Finian's Rainbow evolved out of co-librettist E. Y. Harburg's desire to satirize an economic system that requires gold reserves to be buried in the ground at Fort Knox. This led to the idea of leprechauns and their crock of gold that, according to legend, could grant three wishes. The story takes place in Rainbow Valley, Missitucky, and involves Finian McLonergan, an Irish immigrant, and his efforts to bury a crock of gold which, he is sure will grow and make his rich. Also involved are Og, a leprechaun from whom the crock has been stolen, Finian's daughter, Sharon, who dreams wistfully of Glocca Morra, and Woddy Mahoney, a labor organizer who blames that "Old Devil Moon" for the way he feels about Sharon. A film adaptation was released in 1968, starring Fred Astaire in his last musical role in the movies, and directed by Francis Coppola.

FLOWER DRUM SONG

Music: Richard Rodgers
Lyrics: Oscar Hammerstein II
Book: Oscar Hammerstein II and Joseph Fields
Director: Gene Kelly
Choreographer: Carol Haney
Opened: 12/1/58, New York; a run of 600 performances

It was librettist Joseph Fields who first secured the rights to C. Y. Lee's novel and then approached Rodgers and Hammerstein to join him as collaborators. To dramatize the conflict between the traditionalist older Chinese-Americans living in San Francisco and their thoroughly Americanized offsprings, the musical tells the story of Mei Li, a timid "picture bride" from China, who arrives to fulfill her contract to marry nightclub owner Sammy Fong. Sammy, however, prefers dancer Linda Low (who obviously enjoys being a girl) and the problem is resolved when Sammy's friend Wang Ta discovers that Mei Li is really the bride for him; he sings this volume's "Like a God" to her.

FOLLIES

Music and Lyrics: Stephen Sondheim
Book: James Goldman
Director: Harold Prince
Choreographer: Michael Bennett
Opened: 4/4/71, New York; a run of 522 performances

Taking place at a reunion of former Ziegfeld Follies-type showgirls, the musical deals with the reality of life as contrasted with the unreality of the theatre, a theme it explores through the lives of two couples, the upper class, unhappy Phyllis and Benjamin Stone, and the middle-class, unhappy Sally and Buddy Plummer. *Follies* also depicts these four as they were in their pre-marital youth. Because the show is about the past, and often in flashback, Sondheim purposefully stylized his songs to evoke some of the theatre's great composers and lyricists of the past. A revised version of the show was presented in London in 1987, with some songs replaced with new numbers. "Make the Most of Your Music," Ben's song, comes from the London version. "Beautiful Girls" is sung at the top of the show as the girls make their entrances. *Follies* was given 2 concert performances in 1985 at Avery Fisher Hall in New York City, with a cast that included Barbara Cook, Lee Remick, George Hearn, Mandy Patinkin, Carol Burnett, Licia Albanese, and many others. A new, live recording was released as a result of these performances.

GODSPELL

Music and Lyrics: Stephen Schwartz
Book and Direction: John-Michael Tebelak
Opened: 5/17/71, New York; a run of 2,124 Off-Broadway and then 527 on Broadway

With its rock-flavored score, *Godspell* is a contemporary, flower-child view of the Gospel of St. Matthew, containing dramatized parables of the Prodigal Son, the Good Samaritan, and the Pharisee and the Tax Collector, and with Christ depicted as a clown-faced innocent with a Superman "S" on his shirt. The work originated as a nonmusical play and was first presented at the experimental Café La Mama; after Stephen Schwartz added words and music, the show began it's Off Broadway run at the Cherry Lane Theatre in Greenwich Village, then transferred to the Promenade where it remained for over five years. Beginning in June 1976, it also had a Broadway run. The show was a hit in London as well, and was filmed by Columbia in 1973.

GOOD NEWS

Music: Ray Henderson
Lyrics: B. G. DeSylva and Lew Brown
Book: Laurence Schwab and B. G. DeSylva
Director: Edgar MacGregor
Choreographer: Bobby Connolly
Opened: 9/6/27, New York; a run of 557 performances

Good News inaugurated a series of bright and breezy DeSylva, Brown and Henderson musical comedies that captured the fast-paced spirit of America's flaming youth of the 1920s. In this collegiate caper, the setting is Tait College where the student body is composed of flappers and sheiks, and where the biggest issue is whether the school's football hero will be allowed to play in the big game against Colton despite his failing grade in astronomy. It's all silly, good natured fun. There was an unsuccessful revival on Broadway in 1974. The MGM movie version of 1947 starred June Allyson, Peter Lawford and Mel Tormé.

GRAND HOTEL

Music and Lyrics: Maury Yeston; and Robert Wright and George Forrest
Book: Luther Davis
Director and Choreographer: Tommy Tune
Opened: 11/12/89, New York; a run of 1,018 performances

Based on the novel by Vicki Baum, *Grand Hotel* interweaves the different stories of the staff and guests at a posh Berlin hotel of c. 1930, just as did the well known film of 1932 mixed the stories of Greta Garbo, Lionel Barrymore, Joan Crawford, and a host of others. On Broadway, the stories include the penniless Baron's plans to steal the aging ballerina's jewels but he instead falls in love with her, the businessman who wrestles with his conscience, an aspiring actress who reluctantly peddles her flesh, and the accountant with a zest for living in the face of a fatal disease. Predominantly through dance were the stories intermingled and intersected in the Tommy Tune production.

GREASE

Music, Lyrics and Book: Jim Jacobs and Warren Casey
Director: Tom Moore
Choreographer: Patricia Birch
Opened: 2/14/72, New York; a run of 3,388 performances

A surprise runaway hit reflecting the nostalgia fashion of the 1970s, *Grease* is the story of hip greaser Danny and his whole-some girl Sandy Dumbrowski, a loose plot that serves as an excuse for a light-hearted ride through the early rock 'n' roll of the 1950s. For a number of years, the show was the third longest running Broadway musical, after *A Chorus Line* and *Cats*. The 1978 movie version, starring John Travolta and Olivia Newton-John, is one of the top grossing musical movies of all time.

GUYS AND DOLLS

Music and Lyrics: Frank Loesser
Book: Abe Burrows and Jo Swerling
Director: George S. Kaufman
Choreographer: Michael Kidd
Opened: 11/24/50, New York; a run of 1,200 performances

Populated by the hard-shelled but soft-centered characters who inhabit the world of writer Damon Runyon, this "Musical Fable of Broadway" tells the tale of how Miss Sarah Brown of the Save-a-Soul Mission saves the souls of assorted Times Square riff-raff while losing her heart to the smooth-talking gambler, Sky Masterson. A more comic romance involves Nathan Detroit, who runs the "oldest established permanent floating crap game in New York," and Miss Adelaide, the star of the Hot Box nightclub, to whom he has been engaged for fourteen years, which explains her famous song, "Adelaide's Lament." Because Sky wins a bet, the gamblers are required to attend a service at the mission. In the spirit of things they offer colorful testimonies, the highlight being "Sit Down You're Rockin' the Boat."

Guys and Dolls played on Broadway for 239 performances with an all black cast in 1976. In 1992, an enormously successful revival opened in New York, and a new cast recording was made of the show, with Faith Prince as Miss Adelaide. The 1955 film version stars Frank Sinatra, Marlon Brando, Jean Simmons, and Vivan Blaine (the original Miss Adelaide).

HOW TO SUCCEED IN BUSINESS WITHOUT REALLY TRYING

Music and Lyrics: Frank Loesser
Book: Abe Burrows, based on a play by Jack Weinstock and Willie Gilbert
Director: Abe Burrows
Choreographer: Bob Fosse and Hugh Lambert
Opened: 10/14/61, New York; a run of 1,417 performances

Based on the book by Shepherd Mead, "Business" traces the career of J. Pierpont Finch as he climbs from the mail room to CEO in a few easy steps, not by hard work, but by explicitly following the advice of a book called *How to Succeed in Business Without Really Trying*. Finch is a boyish, charming but ruthless character, a satirical look at the Horatio Alger-ish American myth, with swipes at such business mainstays as the Yes Man, the coffee break, nepotism, the office party, and a boardroom presentation. "I Believe in You" is sung by Finch to his reflection in the mirror of the executive washroom, with a chorus of angry executives in counterpoint. The show won the Pulitzer Prize for drama, the fourth musical ever to do so. A movie version, virtually a filming of the staged production, was released in 1967, again with Robert Morse in the role of Finch.

JEKYLL AND HYDE

Music: Frank Wildhorn
Lyrics and Book: Leslie Bricusse
Director: Robin Phillips
Choreographer: Joey Pizzi
Opened: 4/28/97, New York; a run of 1,543 performances

Based on Robert Louis Stevenson's 1886 novella, *Dr. Jekyll and Mr. Hyde*, this show took nearly a decade to arrive on Broadway. However, the first full score by pop composer Frank Wildhorn was already familiar to most lovers of musical the-atre from two widely circulated concept albums. A North American tour also helped make the show familiar to most of the rest of America before arriving in New York. As in the Stevenson book, a well-meaning scientist, Dr. Henry Jekyll, invents a potion that separates the noble side of man's nature from the evil, bestial side. "This Is the Moment" is the doctor's break-through realization that his theories are possible.

JESUS CHRIST SUPERSTAR

Music: Andrew Lloyd Webber
Lyrics: Tim Rice
Director: Tom O'Horgan
Opened: 10/12/71, New York; a run of 711 performances

Though conceived as a theatre piece, the young team of Lloyd Webber and Rice could not find a producer interested in the "rock opera." Instead, they recorded it as an album, which became a smash hit. Concert tours of the show, which is an eclectic telling of the final week in the life of Jesus, followed, and it didn't take any more convincing that this would fly in the theatre. Despite some mixed press about the production and some objections from religious groups, the piece had its appeal, particularly among the young. The concept of a "rock opera" caused quite a stir at the time.

JOSEPH AND THE AMAZING TECHNICOLOR DREAMCOAT

Music: Andrew Lloyd Webber
Lyrics: Tim Rice
Opened: premiered 1968, London; first revision 1973, London
          11/18/81, New York; a run of 824 performances

The musical lasted all of 15 minutes in its first form, written for a school production in 1968, the first collaboration by the young Lloyd Webber and Rice. By 1973 the piece had been expanded to about 90 minutes, and was given in the West End. The first New York performances took place at the Brooklyn Academy of Music in 1976, and a Broadway run finally commenced in 1981. Somewhat of a forerunner to *Jesus Christ Superstar*, which is also based on Biblical sources, "Joseph" is told entirely in an eclectic mix of song in popular styles such as rock, country, vaudeville, and calypso. From the Old Testament, the story is of Joseph, Jacob's favorite of 12 sons, who is given a remarkable coat of many colors. His jealous brothers sell him into slavery, and he is taken to Egypt, where he interprets the dream of the Pharoah. His wise prophecy so impresses the Pharaoh that Joseph is highly elevated in honor and position and saves the country from famine. The musical has been once again revised in recent years, and a new touring company was launched with the new version in 1992.

MILK AND HONEY

Music and Lyrics: Jerry Herman
Book: Don Appell
Director: Albert Marre
Choreographer: Donald Saddler
Opened: 10/10/61, New York; a run of 543 performances

Milk and Honey was Jerry Herman's first Broadway show. Generally about American tourists in Israel, the show relates the ill-fated romance of a middle-aged businessman and a younger woman who cannot overcome her qualms about a liaison with a married man.

LES MISÉRABLES

Music: Claude-Michel Schönberg
Lyrics: Herbert Kretzmer and Alain Boublil
Original French Text: Alain Boublil and Jean-Marc Natel
Directors: Trevor Nunn and John Caird
Choreographer: Kate Flatt
Opened: 9/80, Paris; an initial run of 3 months
          10/8/85, London
          3/12/87, New York; a run of 6,680 performances

Les Misérables lends a pop opera texture to the 1200 page Victor Hugo epic novel of social injustice and the plight of the downtrodden. The original Parisian version contained only a few songs, and many more were added when the show opened in London. Thus, most of the show's songs were originally written in English. The plot is too rich to capsulize, but centers on Jean Valjean, who has gone to prison in previous years for stealing a loaf of bread, and takes place over several years in the first half of the 19th century. "Bring Him Home" is sung by Jean Valjean about his daughter's fiancé, Marius, as he faces battle in the student uprisings of 1832.

MISS SAIGON

Music: Claude-Michel Schönberg
Lyrics: Richard Maltby, Jr. and Alain Boublil
Director: Nicholas Hynter
Musical Staging: Bob Avian
Opened: 9/20/89, London; a run of 4,264 performances
4/11/91, New York; a run of 4,092 performances

A follow up to their hit *Les Misérables*, *Miss Saigon* is somewhat of an updated telling on the general lines of the Belasco-Puccini tale of Madame Butterfly, only this time the setting is Vietnam during the fall of Saigon at the end of the war. The writers cite a news photograph giving up her child to an American G.I. as the genesis for the idea. The production is noted for a life-size helicopter that descends over the audience. "Why God Why?" is the American soldier Chris' monologue at night in Saigon while the Vietnamese girl Kim is asleep.

THE MYSTERY OF EDWIN DROOD

Music, Lyrics and Book: Rupert Holmes
Director: Wilford Leach
Choreographer: Graciela Daniele
Opened: 12/2/85, New York; a run of 608 performances

The Mystery of Edwin Drood came to Broadway after being intially presented the previous summer in a series of free performances sponsored by the New York Shakespeare Festival at the Delacorte Theatre in Central Park. The impressive score was the first stage work of composer-lyricist-librettist Rupert Holmes, who had previously revealed a talent limited to commercial pop. Holmes' lifelong fascination with Charles Dickens' unfinished novel had been the catalyst for the project. Since there were no clues as to Drood's murderer or even if a murder had been committed, Holmes decided to let the audience provide the show's ending by voting how it turns out. The writer's second major decision was to offer the musical as if it were being performed by an acting company at London's Music Hall Royale in 1873, complete with such conventions as a Chairman (George Rose) to comment on the action and a woman (Betty Buckley) to play the part of Edwin Drood. The show was notable for the appearance of jazz legend Cleo Laine as the eccentric and mysterious Princess Puffer. On November 13, 1986, in an attempt to attract more theatre-goers, the musical's title was changed to *Drood*.

OLIVER!

Music, Lyrics and Book: Lionel Bart
Director: Peter Coe
Opened: 6/30/60, London; a run of 2,618 performances
1/6/63, New York; a run of 744 performances

Oliver! established Lionel Bart as Britain's outstanding musical theatre talent of the 1960s when the musical opened in London. Until overtaken by *Jesus Christ Superstar, Oliver!* set the record as the longest running musical in British history. Based on Charles Dickens; novel about the orphan Oliver Twist and his adventures as one of Fagin's pickpocketing crew, *Oliver!* also had the longest run of any British musical present in New York in the 1960s. The show was revived on Broadway in 1984. In 1968, it was made into an Academy Award winning movie produced by Columbia.

ON A CLEAR DAY YOU CAN SEE FOREVER

Music: Burton Lane
Lyrics and Book: Alan Jay Lerner
Director: Robert Lewis
Choreographer: Herbert Ross
Opened: 10/17/65, New York; a run of 280 performances

Alan Jay Lerner's fascination with the phenomenon of extrasensory perception led to his teaming with composer Richard Rodgers in 1962 to write a musical to be called *I Picked a Daisy*. When that didn't work out, Lerner turned to composer Burton Lane, with whom he had worked in Hollywood years before. The result is a show about Daisy Gamble, who can not only predict the future, but under hypnosis, by Dr. Mark Bruckner, can recall her past life as Melinda Wells in 18th century London. Mark becomes infatuated with Melinda, who becomes a romantic rival to the present day Daisy. They split up, but he persuades her to "Come Back to Me." Barbra Streisand starred in the 1970 Vincente Minnelli filmed version of the musical.

THE PHANTOM OF THE OPERA

Music: Andrew Lloyd Webber
Lyrics: Charles Hart, Richard Stilgoe
Book: Richard Stilgoe and Andrew Lloyd Webber
Director: Harold Prince
Choreographer: Gillian Lynne
Opened: October 9, 1986, London
             January 26, 1988, New York

The most financially successful musical in history is based on the French novel *Le Fantome de l'Opera*, published in 1911. It is the story of a disfigured musical genius who haunts the trackless catacombs beneath the Paris Opera. The world's revulsion at his outer ugliness twists the artist within. He conceives a passion for a lovely young singer, Christine Daaé, and hypnotizes her into becoming his student and worshipper. The Phantom's spell is broken with the arrival of a young man who vies with the Phantom for Christine's affections, and the Phantom turns murderous. The production's most famous element is a chandelier that falls from above the audience and crashes onto the stage. "Think of Me" is sung by Christine near the top of the show. It builds from a pretty melody sung at an audition, to the full operatic treatment on Christine's opening night, after replacing the ailing leading lady. "Wishing You Were Somehow Here Again" is Christine's plea at her father's grave, after the Phantom's threat begins to grow.

PLAIN AND FANCY

Music: Albert Hague
Lyrics: Arnold B. Horwitt
Book: Joseph Stein and Will Glickman
Director: Morton Da Costa
Choreographer: Helen Tamiris
Opened: 1/27/55, New York; a run of 461 performances

The setting of *Plain and Fancy* was Amish country in Pennsylvania, where two worldly New Yorkers (Richard Derr and Shirl Conway) have gone to sell a farm they had inherited—but not before they had a chance to meet the God-fearing people and appreciate their simple but unyielding way of living. The warm and atmospheric score was composed by Albert Hague, familiar to television viewers as the bearded music teacher in the series *Fame*.

THE SECRET GARDEN

Music: Lucy Simon
Lyrics and Book: Marsha Norman
Director: Susan H. Schulman
Choreographer: Michael Lichtefeld
Opened: 4/25/91, New York; 706 performances

Based on the novel by Frances Hodgson Burnett, the story is of an orphaned Mary Lennox, who is sent to live with her uncle Archibald in Yorkshire. He is absorbed in grief over the death of his young wife 10 years earlier, and the house is gloomy and mysterious. Mary finds her dead aunt's "secret garden," passionately nurtures it to life, and Archie also comes back to life. "A Bit of Earth" is Archibald's monologue musing at Mary's request for a garden to tend. Mandy Patinkin first played the role. "Winter's on the Wing" is sung by the gardener about the coming spring.

SHE LOVES ME

Music: Jerry Bock
Lyrics: Sheldon Harnick
Book: Joe Masteroff
Director: Harold Prince
Choreographer: Carol Haney
Opened: 4/23/63, New York; a run of 301 performances

The closely integrated, melody drenched score of *She Loves Me* is certainly one of the best ever written for a musical comedy. It was based on a Hungarian play, *Parfumerie,* by Miklos Laszlo, that had already been used as the basis for two films, *The Shop Around the Corner* and, adapted to an American setting, *In the Good Old Summertime.* Set in the 1930s in what could only be Budapest, the tale is of the people who work in Maraczek's Parfumerie, principally the constantly quabbling sales clerk Amalia Balash (Barbara Cook) and the manager Georg Nowack (Daniel Massey). It is soon revealed that they are anonymous pen pals who agree to meet one night at the Café Imperiale, though neither knows the other's identity. In "Tonight at Eight" Georg anxiously awaits their first face to face meeting. That evening he realizes that it is Amalia who is waiting for him in the restaurant, but doesn't let on, teasing her some with "Tango Tragique." In "She Loves Me" he realizes that though Amalia loves him, she just doesn't know yet who it is. Eventually, he is emboldened to reveal his identity by quoting from one of Amalia's letters. *She Loves Me,* which would have starred Julie Andrews had she not been filming *Mary Poppins,* was one of Barbara Cook's most magical portrayals. The show is well represented on the original cast album, which on two disks preserves practically every note of the show's music.

THE STUDENT PRINCE

Music: Sigmund Romberg
Lyrics and Book: Dorothy Donnelly
Director: J. C. Huffman
Opened: 12/2/24, New York; a run of 608 performances

Though the popularity of operetta had yielded to more up to date musical comedy, *The Student Prince in Heidelberg* (the complete title was used throughout its initial run) was the longest running musical of the 1920s. It was one of the last of the American operettas that was written to sound as if it had been translated from a European language. Set in 1860, the sentimental story is of Prince Karl Franz who has gone to Heidelberg with his tutor to complete his education. He meets a waitress at an inn, and in boy-meets-girl tradition the two are soon singing love duets. Duty calls, however, and the Prince has to tear himself away to become king. A few years later he returns to Heidelberg looking for his lost youth. The show was very popular in its time, touring the country for eight years, with Broadway revivals in 1931 and 1943. A silent film version was released in 1927, and in 1954, with Mario Lanza's singing voice, another film production was released. The piece has entered the repertory of several opera companies.

FORBIDDEN FRUIT
(THE APPLE TREE)
from *The Apple Tree*

Misterioso

Words and Music by JERRY BOCK
and SHELDON HARNICK

SNAKE:
Lis-ten close-ly.

[Vamp ad lib.]

Let me fill you in —— A-bout the rich, ripe, round, red,
sweet and juic - y

Ros-y ap-ples they call for-bid-den fruit;_ What I'm a-
Lus cious bite_ of this not for-bid-den fruit;_ You'll see your

left for you and me.
will be o-ver-joyed

Now in the ave - rage ap - ple
When he be-comes a - ware of

You're ac - cust - omed to skin, seeds, flesh and core.
Your at - tain-ments, he'll beam with lov-ing pride,

But you will
And he will

find that these are
say: "Oh, Eve, you're

Spe-cial ap - ples that give you some-thing more,
In - dis pen - sa-ble--- please don't leave my side."

Why ev - 'ry seed con - tains some in-for-ma - tion you
And with your nif - ty, new - found ed - u - ca - tion, he'll

f

cresc. poco a poco

I MET A GIRL

from *Bells Are Ringing*

Lyrics by BETTY COMDEN
and ADOLPH GREEN
Music by JULE STYNE

But so what, what ___ has she got oth-

___ ers have not? _____ Two eyes, two lips, a

nose _____ most girls have some of those. _____

___ Yet when she looks ___ up at

22

me, what do I see? The most en-chant-ing face. My pulse be-gins to race. Hey! I met a girl, a mar-vel-ous girl! She's rar-er than u-ran-i-um and fair-er than a pearl. I

MAYBE I SHOULD CHANGE MY WAYS

from *Beggar's Holiday*

Words and Music by JOHN LaTOUCHE
and DUKE ELLINGTON

WILLKOMMEN
from *Cabaret*

Lyrics by FRED EBB
Music by JOHN KANDER

Hap - py to see you, blei - be, res - te, stay.

Will - kom - men, bien - ve - nue, _ wel - come, Im Cab - a - ret, _

au Cab - a - ret, _ to Cab - a -

ret. _____

8va --------------------

8va --------------------

ONCE UPON A TIME TODAY

from *Call Me Madam*

Words and Music by
IRVING BERLIN

To a twen-ti-eth cen-tury fair-y tale.

Once _____ there was a prin-cess, once _____ there was a guy

And _____ they fell in love one won-der-ful day. _____

But _____ she was a prin-cess, He _____ was just a guy

So _____ there was the roy - al dev - il to pay _____ They were

or - dered not to speak to one an - oth - er _____ And they knew the sor - row that would bring _

_ Still they prom - ised not to speak to one an - oth - er. _____ But they

did - n't prom - ise not to sing. __ So _____ be - neath her win - dow

found that when he set them all to mus-ic _____ They were just as good as po-et-ry

So _____ be-neath her win - dow ten - der-ly he sang

"How _____ a - bout that hap-py end-ing in May?" _____

Once _____ up-on a time to - day. _____

ANTHEM
from *Chess*

Words and Music by
BENNY ANDERSSON, TIM RICE
and BJORN ULVAEUS

Andante cantabile (*like a hymn*)

ANATOLY:

No man, ____ no mad-ness, though their sad pow-er may pre-vail, can pos-

sess, con - quer my coun-try's heart, they rise to fail. ____

She is _____ e - ter - nal, long be - fore na-tion lines were drawn, _____ when no

flags flew and no ar - mies stood, my land _____ was born. _____ And

you ask me why I love her through wars, death and des - pair.

She is the con - stant, we who don't care _____ And

you won-der will I leave her – but how?

poco mosso

I cross ov - er bor - ders but I'm still ____ there now. ____

How can I leave her? ____ Where would I start? ____

Let man's ___ pet-ty na-tions tear them-selves ____ a-

part. _____ My land's ___ on-ly bor-der lies a-

round ____ my heart. _____

WHERE I WANT TO BE
from *Chess*

Words and Music by BENNY ANDERSSON,
TIM RICE and BJÖRN ULVAEUS

Nearly like a waltz (not too slow); like a music box
ANATOLY:

Who needs a dream?

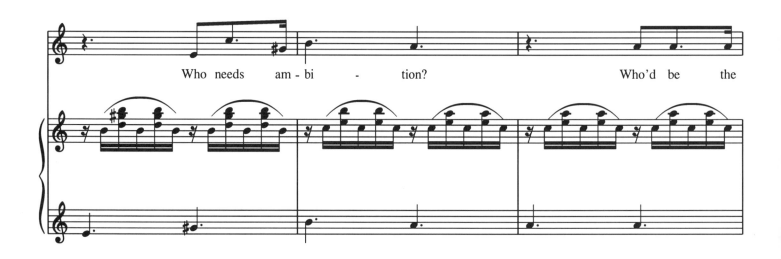

Who needs am-bi - tion? Who'd be the

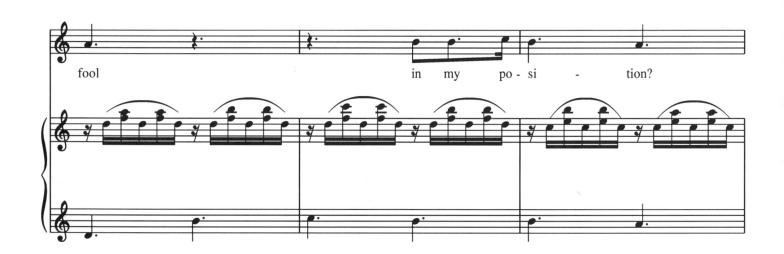

fool in my po-si - tion?

When the cra - zy wheel slows down, where will I be? Back where I start - ed. Don't get me wrong, I'm not com-plain - ing.

Times have been good, fast, en - ter -

tain - ing. But what's the point

if I'm con - ceal - ing most of my

thoughts all of my feel - ing.

poco rit.

p

GERANIUMS IN THE WINDER
from *Carousel*

Lyrics by OSCAR HAMMERSTEIN II
Music by RICHARD RODGERS

Mr. Snow: *(spoken)* Leave me to my shattered dreams.
They are all I have left, memories of what didn't happen.

Molto moderato *(slowy)*

MR. SNOW:

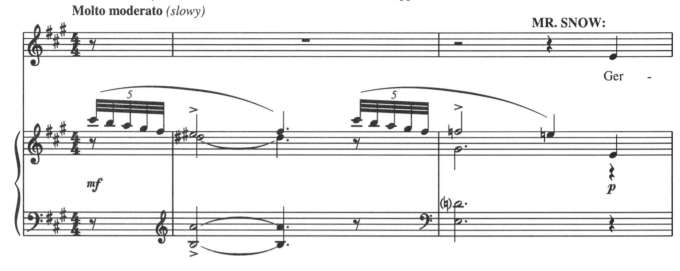

Ger -

(broad and emphatically)

an - i - ums in the win - der, Hy - dran - geas on the lawn, And

break - fast in the kit - chen In the tim - id pink of dawn, And

you to __ blow me kiss - es When I head - ed fer the sea. We

might hev been a hap - py pair of lov - ers, Might - n't hev

we? And

com - in' __ home at twi - light It might hev been so

sweet   To take my ketch of her - ring   And

lay them at   your feet!   I   might hev ___ had a

ba - by,   To dan - dle on my knee,   But   all these things That

might hev been, are nev - er, nev - er to   be!

I KNOW ABOUT LOVE

from *Do Re Mi*

Lyrics by BETTY COMDEN
and ADOLPH GREEN
Music by JULE STYNE

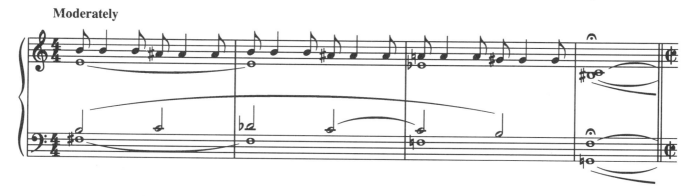

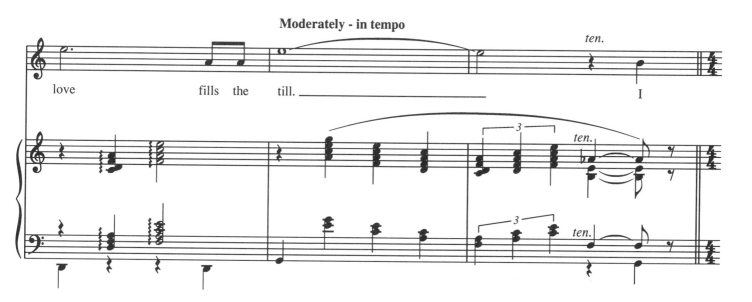

54

mov - ies I've seen, _____ When love fill the screen, _____ Then the

fi - re-works flare, vi - o - lins fill the air, The un - i - verse reels. _____ For

love's a mag - ic spell, It's what makes mu - sic sell. I

know all a - bout it, All ex - cept how it feels. _____

ASKING FOR YOU
from *Do Re Mi*

Lyrics by BETTY COMDEN
and ADOLPH GREEN
Music by JULE STYNE

Moderately Slow

WHEELER:

I'm not

Poco più mosso

ask - ing _____ for a dance. _____ I'm not

ask - ing _____ for ro - mance. _____ From this

mo - ment, _____ send - ing flow - ers, _____ Those stol - en

ho - urs _____ just won't do. _____ I'm not

look - ing _____ for a fling. _____ That's for

chil - dren _____ drunk with spring. _____ What I

ask for _____ is love for ev - er, _____ Yes, for

ev - er, _____ all life through. _____ I'm just

ask - ing _____ for you. _____

MARGOT
from *The Desert Song*

Lyrics by OTTO HARBACH
and OSCAR HAMMERSTEIN II
Music by SIGMUND ROMBERG

HIGH FLYING, ADORED
from *Evita*

Lyrics by TIM RICE
Music by ANDREW LLOYD WEBBER

Moderato

CHE: High fly-ing, a - dored. _ So young, _____ the in - stant queen, _ a rich beau-ti - ful thing, _ of all the tal - ents _ a cross be - tween _ a fan - ta - sy of the bed - room, and a saint. And

The right hand part of piano is a simple suggestion of the kind of improvisation that is appropriate in this song.

ON THIS NIGHT OF A THOUSAND STARS

from *Evita*

Lyrics by TIM RICE
Music by ANDREW LLOYD WEBBER

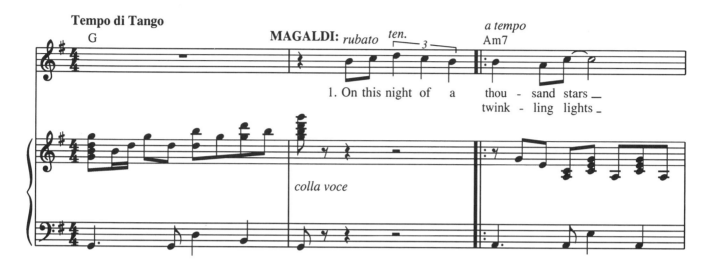

In the score of *Evita*, the pianist is directed to "ad lib. (corny night club, Spanish style)."
The right hand in this edition is a simple, written out improvisation.

I LIKE YOU
from *Fanny*

Words and Music by
HAROLD ROME

MIRACLE OF MIRACLES

from *Fiddler on the Roof*

Music by JERRY BOCK
Words by SHELDON HARNICK

Allegro, quasi agitato

MOTEL:

Won - der of won - ders, mir - a - cle of mir - a - cles, God took a Dan - iel

once a - gain. Stood by his side and mir - a - cle of mir - a - cles,

That was a mir-a-cle, too. But of all God's mir-a-cles, large and small, The

most mi-rac-u-lous one of all Is that out of a worth-less lump of clay,

God has made a man to-day! _____

Won-der of won-ders, mir-a-cle of mir-a-cles, God took a tai-lor

too. But of all God's mir - a - cles, large and small, The
most mi - rac - u - lous one of all Is the one I thought could nev - er be:
God has giv - en you to
me!

LIKE A GOD

from *Flower Drum Song*

Lyrics by OSCAR HAMMERSTEIN II
Music by RICHARD RODGERS

man that I was be - fore.

Refrain

Like a god with my head a - bove the trees, I can walk with a

(Str., W.W.)

god - like stride._____ With a step I can

clear the sev - en seas, When I know_ you are by_ my side._

— Like a god with a moun-tain in my hand And my

arm thrown a - round the sky,_ All the

Like a god I can tear a-way the mist from the sky if you want it blue. In the wake of the mist Like a god-dess you'll be kissed By a god in love with you.

Like a God with a moun - tain in my hand And my

arm thrown a - round the sky, _____

All the world can be mine at my com - mand, When you're

near ___ and I hear ___ you sigh. _____

OLD DEVIL MOON
from *Finian's Rainbow*

Lyrics by E. Y. HARBURG
Music by BURTON LANE

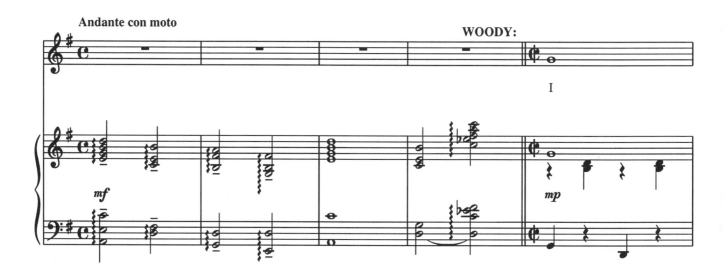

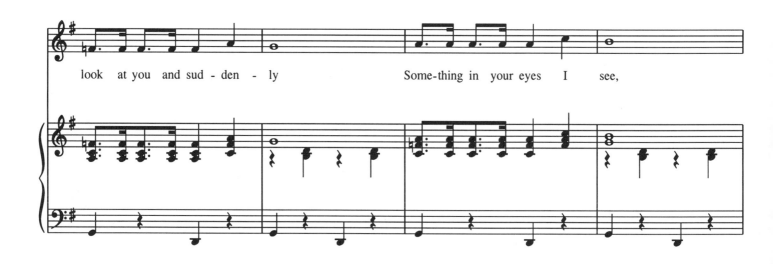

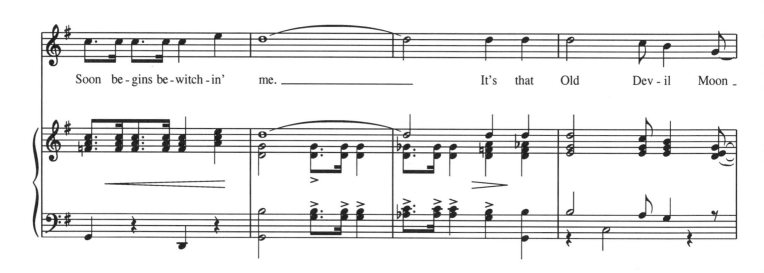

got me fly - in' high and wide On a mag - ic car - pet ride,

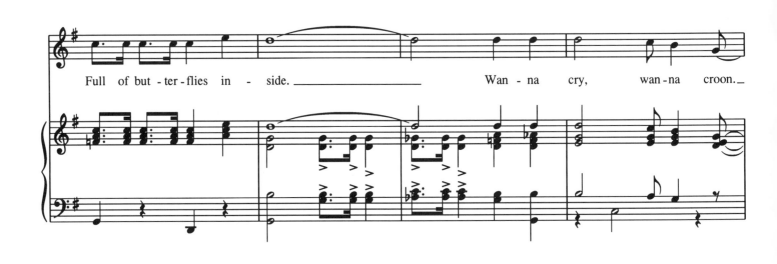

Full of but - ter - flies in - side. _____ Wan - na cry, wan - na croon. __

__ Wan - na laugh like a loon. __ It's that Old Dev - il Moon __

in your eyes. ___ Just when I think I'm ___

free as a dove, ___ Old Dev - il Moon, deep in your

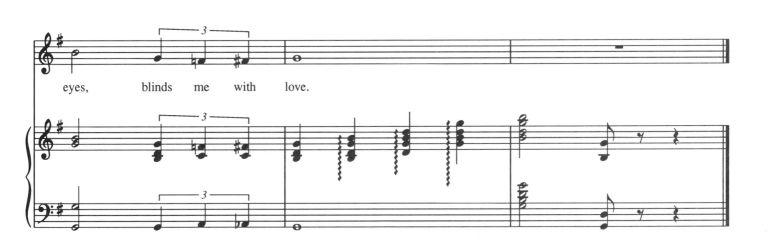

eyes, blinds me with love.

BEAUTIFUL GIRLS

from *Follies*

Words and Music by
STEPHEN SONDHEIM

Moderately
ROSCOE:

Hats off, here they come, those Beau-ti-ful girls.

That's what you've been wait-ing for.

Na - ture nev-er fash-ioned a flow-er so fair.

No rose can com - pare, Noth - ing re - spec - ta - ble

half so de - lec - ta - ble. Cheer them in their glo - ry, Dia - monds and

pearls, Dazz - ling jew - els by the score.

This is what beau - ty can be,

Beau -ty ce -les -tial, the best, you'll a -gree: All for you, these beau -ti -ful

girls! _____

Care -ful, here's the home of Beau -ti -ful girls,

Where your rea -son is un -done. _____

Tpts.

Beau - ty can't be hin - dered from tak - ing its toll.

You may ___ lose con - trol. Faced with these Lo - re - leis,

What man can mor - al - ize? Cau - tion, on your guard with

Beau - ti - ful girls, Flaw - less charm - ers ev - 'ry -

LOVE CAN'T HAPPEN

from *Grand Hotel*

Words and Music by
MAURY YESTON

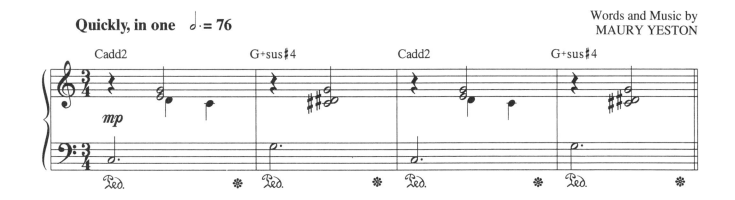

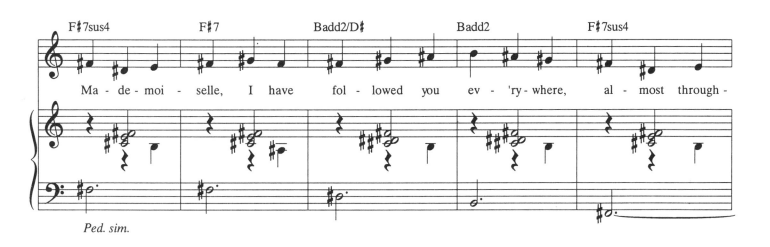

Ma - de - moi - selle, I have fol - lowed you ev - 'ry - where, al - most through-

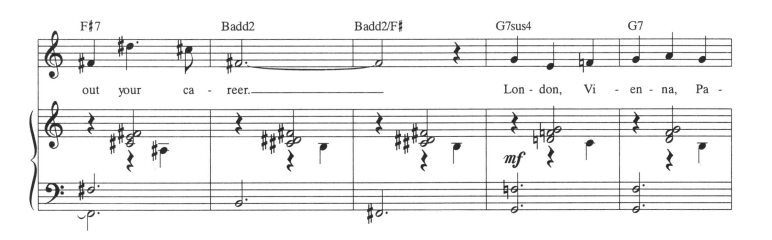

out your ca - reer._____ Lon - don, Vi - en - na, Pa -

AT THE GRAND HOTEL

from *Grand Hotel*

Words and Music by
MAURY YESTON

Warmly ♩ = 104

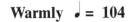

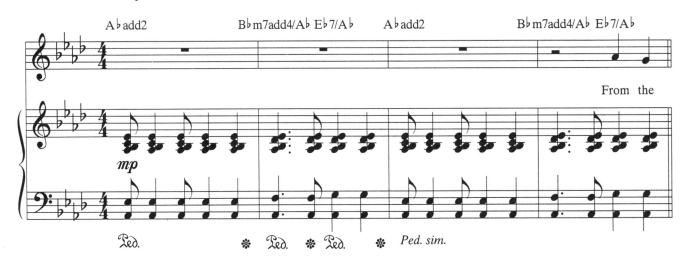

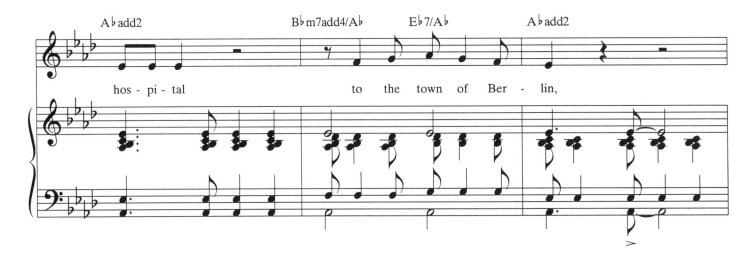

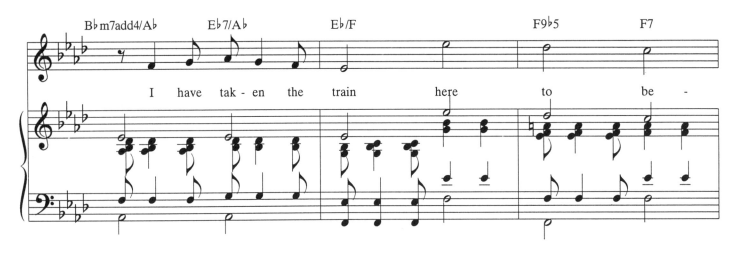

ALL GOOD GIFTS

from *Godspell*

Words and Music by
STEPHEN SCHWARTZ

111

LUCKY IN LOVE
from *Good News*

Words and Music by B. G. DeSYLVA,
LEW BROWN and RAY HENDERSON

I don't ev - er gam - ble,   Sweet - heart, I re -
Play - ing cards and lov - ing,   May be lots of

fuse.   Not be - cause I hate to,
fun.   Some - thing seems to tell me

118

ALONE AT THE DRIVE-IN MOVIE

from *Grease*

Lyric and Music by WARREN CASEY
and JIM JACOBS

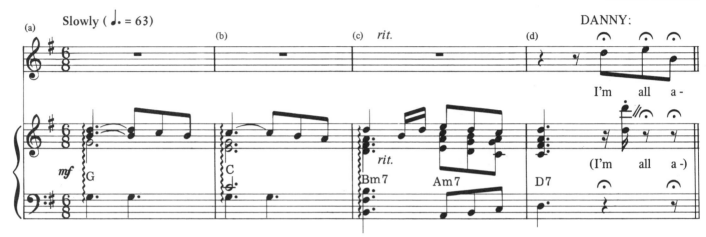

back seat,_____ all a-lone_____ just ain't

too neat,_____ at the pas - sion pit want-ing

you._____ And when the

125

SIT DOWN YOU'RE ROCKIN' THE BOAT

from *Guys And Dolls*

By FRANK LOESSER

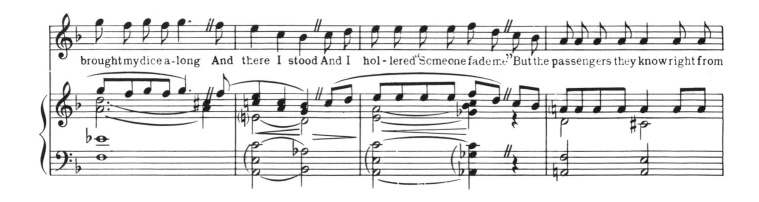

der — By the sharp la-pel of your checkered coat Sit down — sit down sit down —

— sit down sit down — you're rockin' the boat —

Freely

sailed a-way on that lit-tle boat to Heaven And by some chance found a bot-tle in my fist And

there I stood, nicely passin' out the whiskey But the pas-sen-gers were bound to re-sist For the

I ONLY WANT TO SAY
(GETHSEMANE)
from *Jesus Christ Superstar*

Lyrics by TIM RICE
Music by ANDREW LLOYD WEBBER

MCA music publishing

start

I BELIEVE IN YOU
from *How to Succeed in Business Without Really Trying*

Music & Lyrics by
FRANK LOESSER

In 1 — FINCH:
Now there you are, ___ Yes, there's that face; ___

In 2
That face that some - how I trust. ___ It

Swing - In 2
may em - bar - rass you to hear me say it, But say it I must,

Note: Finch is addressing himself in the song.

with self-assurance

say it I must! You have the cool,

clear eyes of a seek - er of wis - dom and truth;

Yet, there's that up - turned

chin, And the grin of im - pet - u - ous youth.

brave spring of the ti - ger that quick - ens your walk.

religioso e molto legato

Oh, I be - lieve in you, _____

I be - lieve in you. _____

In 2

And when my faith in my fel - low man _____

seek-er of wis-dom and truth; Yet, with the

slam, bang, tang rem - i - nis-cent of gin and ver-mouth,

religioso e molto legato

Oh, I be - lieve in you, _____

Oh, I be - lieve in you. _____

(rit.)

THIS IS THE MOMENT

from *Jekyll & Hyde*

Lyrics by LESLIE BRICUSSE
Music by FRANK WILDHORN

This is the key of the concept cast recording. The Broadway key is E-flat.

CLOSE EVERY DOOR

from *Joseph and the Amazing*
Technicolor Dreamcoat

Lyrics by TIM RICE
Music by ANDREW LLOYD WEBBER

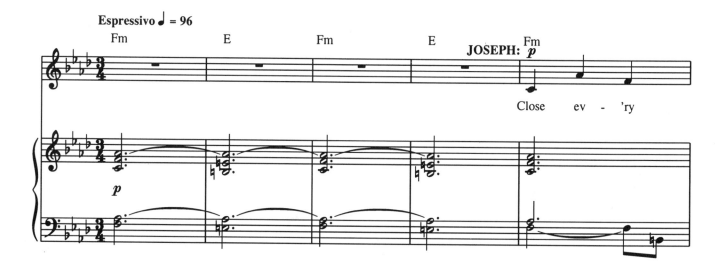

WHY GOD WHY?

from *Miss Saigon*

Music and Lyrics by CLAUDE-MICHEL SCHÖNBERG,
ALAIN BOUBLIL and RICHARD MALTBY JR.

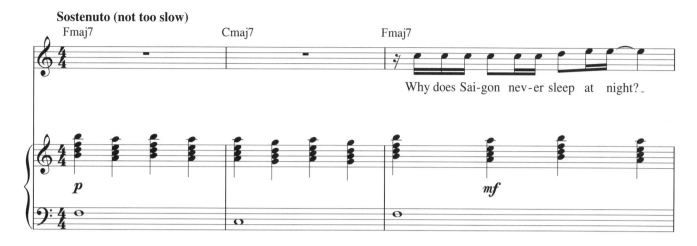

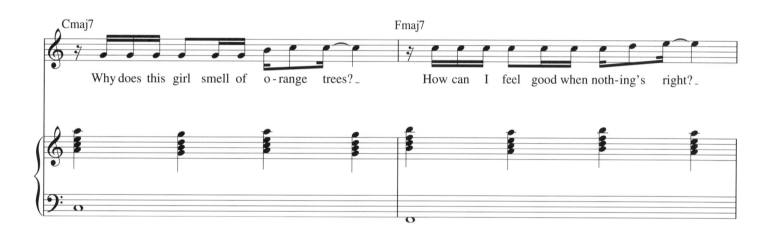

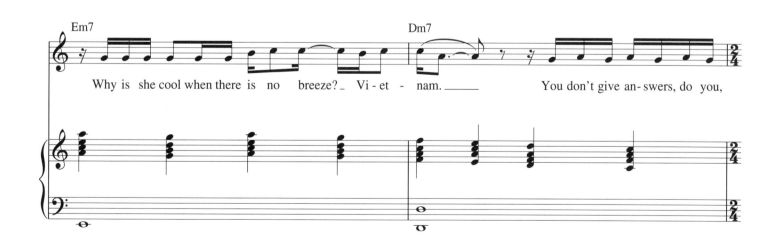

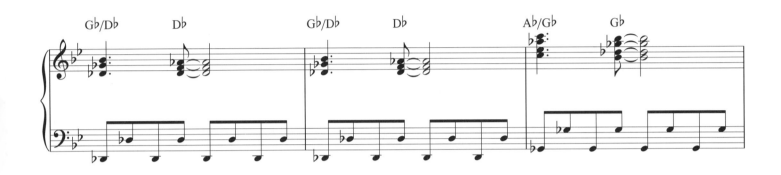

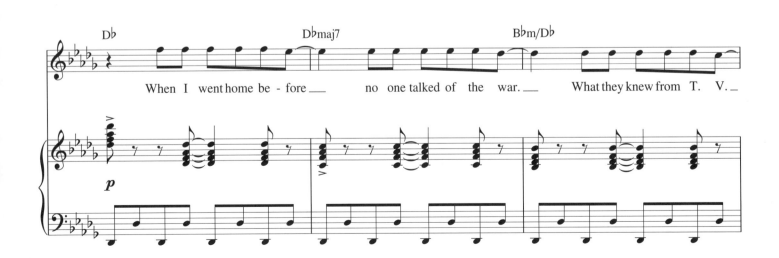

When I went home be - fore ___ no one talked of the war. ___ What they knew from T. V. ___

in this place?_ I liked my mem-'ries as they were_ but

now I'll leave_ re-mem-b'ring her, just her._____

I WILL FOLLOW YOU

from *Milk And Honey*

Music and Lyric by
JERRY HERMAN

Rubato

DAVID:

In my grey flan-nel suit, In my new shin-y car, In my split lev-el house, With my big black ci-gar, Can't you

I will fol-low you, I am rea-dy to Go where-ev-er you hap-pen to lead me.

Just in case you should hap-pen to need me All that you'll have to do Is turn a-round for

Faster

I'll be fol-low-ing you.

BRING HIM HOME

from *Les Misérables*

Lyrics by HERBERT KRETZMER
and ALAIN BOUBLIL
Music by CLAUDE-MICHEL SCHÖNBERG

170

JASPER'S CONFESSION
from *The Mystery of Edwin Drood*

Words and Music by
RUPERT HOLMES

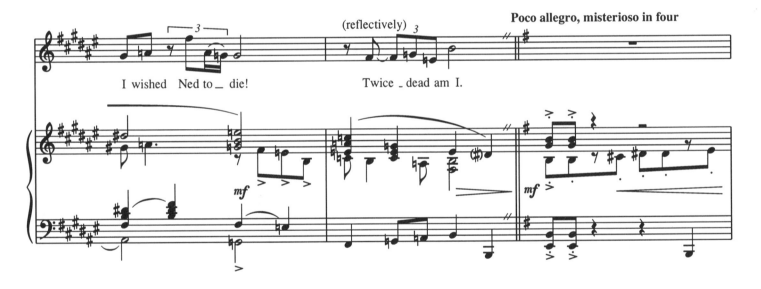

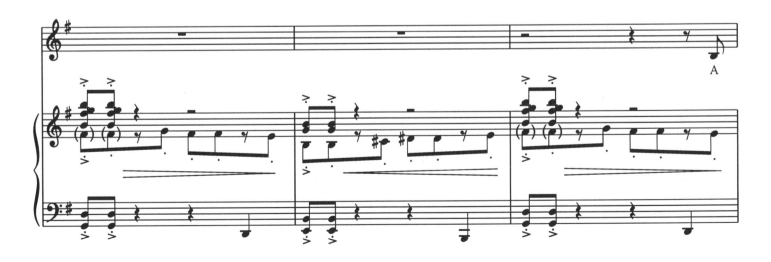

man could split in twain, yet to all eyes re-main a soul gen-teel who can con-ceal the

ven-om in his brain. And if he draws up-on the pause in mad-ness o-pium smoke sup-

plies — why this great sur-prise? There are two men in me, and

cun-ning bright is he who hides him-self, re-sides him-self where I've no eyes to see. But

now I think he's at the brink of break-ing through the door— I'm in, he's out, I'm

out, he's free, I'm free. I'm me once more! How man-y times I've killed that

ad lib., faster

drood up-on my flights! My flights that burst the smug pre-sump-tion of his rights—

his rights as heir, his rights to share my Ro-sa's bed. It took no smoke for me to

SHE WASN'T YOU

from *On a Clear Day You Can See Forever*

Words by ALAN JAY LERNER
Music by BURTON LANE

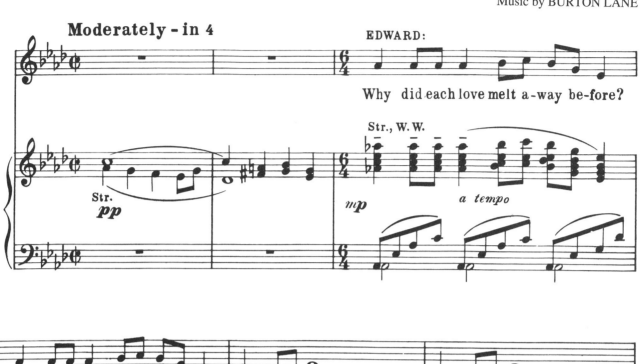

178

why each af-fair al-ways fad-ed so fast.

On-ly with you was I born to live; On-ly to you is the love I give,

Love for as long as a life-time can last.

BOY FOR SALE
from the Columbia Pictures-Romulus film *Oliver!*

Music and Lyrics by
LIONEL BART

stout. If I should say he was-n't ver-y greed-y I

could not, I'd be tell-ing you a tale. One boy Boy for

sale _____ Come take a peep Have you ev-er seen as Nice a boy for

(Spoken:) Liberal terms, Mister Sowerberry, - Liberal terms.

sale.

YOUNG AND FOOLISH

from *Plain And Fancy*

Words by ARNOLD B. HORWITT
Music by ALBERT HAGUE

Slowly

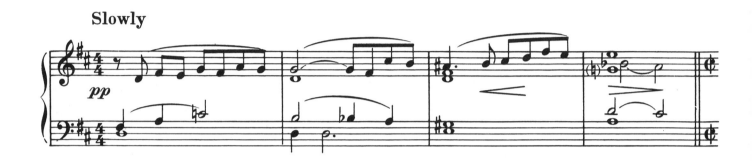

Con moto

Once we were fool-ish chil-dren, Play-ing as chil-dren play.

Rac-ing thro' a mea-dow A-pril bright, Dream-ing on a hill-top half the night.

care - free days, The sun - lit days go by. Soon e - nough the

blue-bird has to fly. _____ We were fool - ish,

One day we fell in love, Now we won - der What we were

dream - ing of, Smil - ing in the sun - light, Laugh - ing in the

rain, I wish that we were young and fool-ish a - gain.

rall. accel.

pp più mosso (in 2)

(tempo I)

Smil - ing in the sun - light, Laugh - ing in the rain, I

wish that we were young and fool-ish a - gain.

rit.

ff

A BIT OF EARTH
from *The Secret Garden*

Lyrics by MARSHA NORMAN
Music by LUCY SIMON

old, _____ and does-n't care if one small girl wants things to grow. _____

rit.   *a tempo-flowing*
mp   *a tempo-flowing*

She needs a   friend.   She needs a   fa - ther, broth-er, sis - ter, moth-er's

arms _____   She needs to   laugh. _____   She needs to

dance and learn to work her girl - ish   charms _____   She needs a

home _____ The on - ly thing she real - ly needs, I can - not give _____

In - stead she asks a bit of earth to make it

live.

She should have a po - ny

WINTER'S ON THE WING
from *The Secret Garden*

Lyrics by MARSHA NORMAN
Music by LUCY SIMON

*Play all grace notes on the beat.

You'll be here to see it Stand and

breathe it all the day.

Stoop and feel it, Stop and hear it

Spring, I say._____ I say be-

gone ye howl-ing gales,— Be off ye frost-y morns.

All ye sol-id streams be-gin to thaw.

Melt, ye wat-er-falls,— Part, ye fro-zen win-ter walls—

See, see now— it's start - ing And now the

Mist is lift-ing high, leav-in' bright blue air roll-in' clear 'cross the moor. Comes the May, I say. The

storm-'ll soon be by leav-in' clear blue sky, Soon the sun will shine, Comes the day, say I. And

You'll be here to see it. Stand and

breathe it all ___ the day

Stoop and feel it, stop and hear it

Spring _____ I _____

say! _____

TONIGHT AT EIGHT
from *She Loves Me*

Lyrics by SHELDON HARNICK
Music by JERRY BOCK

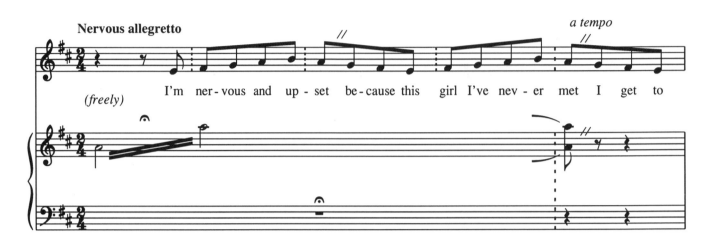

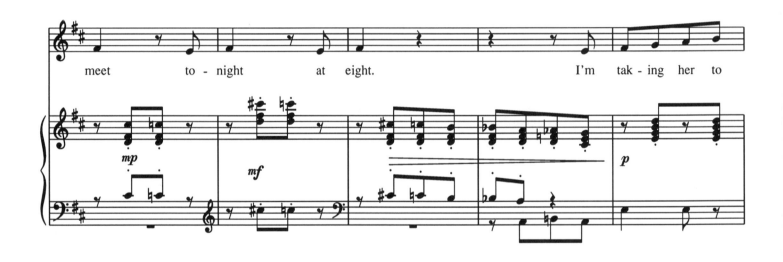

eight. It's ear-ly in the morn-ing and our date is not till

eight o-'clock to-night, and yet al-read-y I can see _____

What a night-mare this whole day will be. _____

I have-n't slept a wink, I on-ly think of our ap-

writ - ten, she may not be ver - y smit - ten and my hopes per - haps may

all col - lapse ka - put! to - night at eight.

I wish I knew ex - act - ly how I'll act and what will hap-pen when we

dine to - night at eight. I know I'll drop the

204

TANGO TRAGIQUE
from *She Loves Me*

Lyrics by SHELDON HARNICK
Music by JERRY BOCK

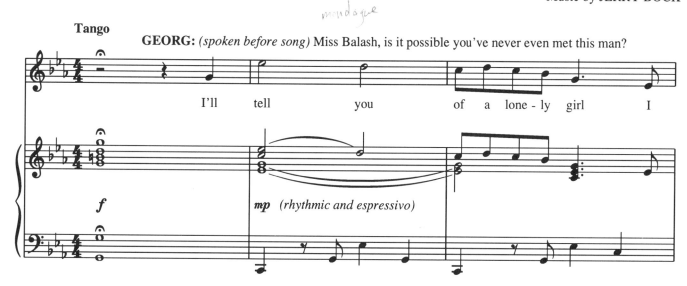

GEORG: *(spoken before song)* Miss Balash, is it possible you've never even met this man?

I'll tell you of a lone-ly girl I knew.

Her sto-ry I fear is tra-gic to hear.

Nev-er-the-less it's true. Her

down-fall, as I now re-call be-gan

When her lone-ly hearts club found her a lone-ly

man. She sat down and wrote, he

an-swered her note, and now there was no re-treat. Then

that day she was nev-er seen a - round. _____ We

searched high and low but search as we would on - ly a trace was found. Her

left leg float-ing in a lo - cal brook. We

nev-er could find the rest of her or her book.

SHE LOVES ME

from *She Loves Me*

Lyrics by SHELDON HARNICK
Music by JERRY BOCK

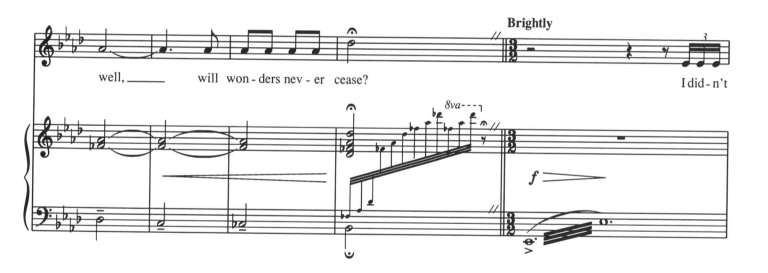

have her. I nev-er knew her, but now I do, and I could, and I would, and I

Moderately bright

know _____ She

loves me. And to my a-maze-ment I love it

know-ing that she loves me. She loves me. True, she does-n't

show it. How could she when she does-n't know it.

Yes - ter - day she loathed me. *Bah!* Now to-day she likes. me. *Hah!* And to-mor-row

to - mor - row, __ Ah! _____

My teeth ache from the urge to touch her. I'm

Yes-ter-day I loathed her. *Bah!* Now to-day I love her. *Hah!* And to-mor-row,

to - mor - row __ Ah! _____

__ I'm ting - ling such de-li - cious tin - gels. I'm

trem - bling, what the hell does that mean? I'm freez - ing

that's be-cause it's cold out. But still I'm in-can-des-cent, and like some ad - o - les-cent, I'd like to scrawl on ev - 'ry wall I see. ___ ___ She loves me! ___ She loves me! ___

SERENADE
from *The Student Prince*

Lyrics by DOROTHY DONNELLY
Music by SIGMUND ROMBERG

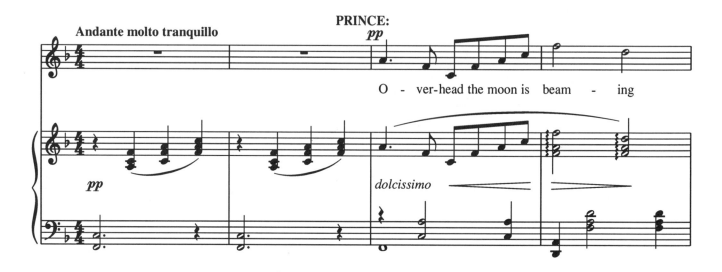

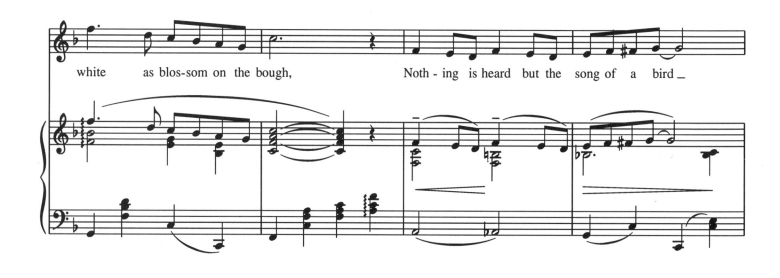

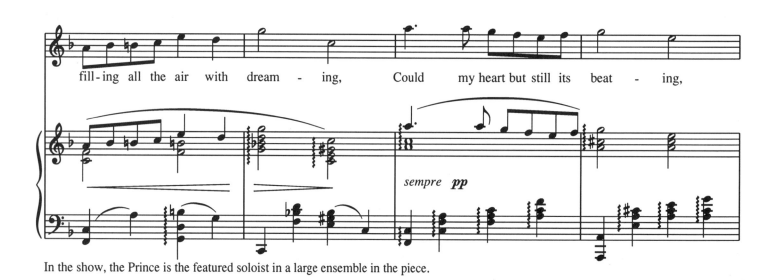

In the show, the Prince is the featured soloist in a large ensemble in the piece.

heart must tell you that I am near, Lean from a-bove while I

pour out my love, for you know to my life you are dear, Oh

hear ____ my long-ing cry; oh love ____ me or I die!

Tempo I

O - ver-head the moon is beam - ing

White as blos-soms on the bough, Noth-ing is heard but the

song of a bird___ fill-ing all the air with dream - ing,

Could my heart but still its beat - ing, on - ly you can tell it how, ___ be-lov-ed!

From your win-dow give me greet - ing, I swear my e-ter - nal vow!

*This is the original phrasing. Another option is to breathe after "swear," and not break in the middle of the word "eternal" (perhaps after it, before "vow.")

THE MUSIC OF THE NIGHT

from *The Phantom of the Opera*

Music by ANDREW LLOYD WEBBER
Lyrics by CHARLES HART
Additional lyrics by RICHARD STILGOE

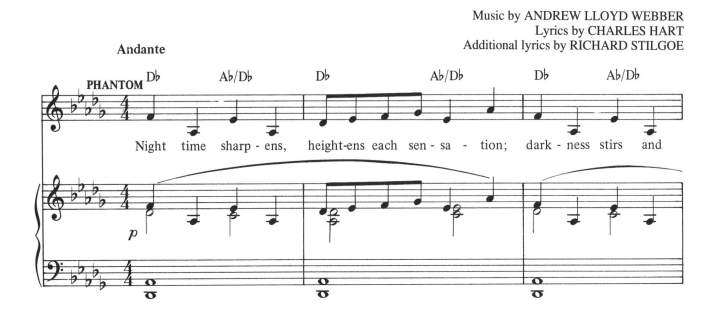

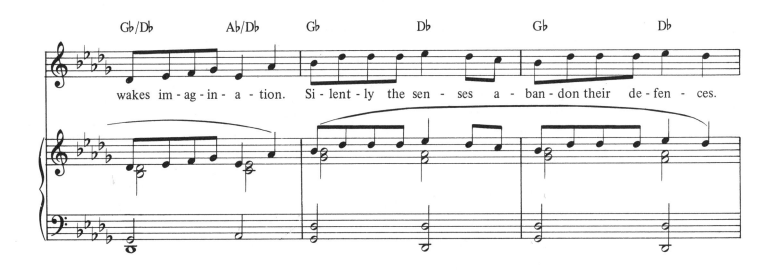

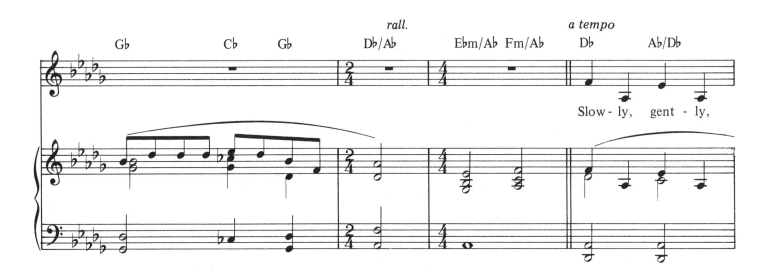